WHAT IT IS

Esther Jansma studied philosophy at the University of Amsterdam, later specialising in ecological archaeology, obtaining her doctorate for research in dendrochronology. She works as an archaeologist, and is currently senior researcher at Dutch Heritage. She holds a Chair in Dendrochronology at Utrecht University. In 2004 she took part in the Writing on the Wall project, a five-year international programme involving writers from the north of England, Scotland and countries which originally garrisoned Hadrian's Wall. *What It Is* (Bloodaxe Books, 2008) is the first English translation of her work, drawing on all the collections she has published in the Netherlands and including poems inspired by parts of the Wall where where Friesian and Schelt Auxiliaries were stationed.

She published her first book of poems, *Stem onder mijn bed* (Voice Under My Bed), in 1988, followed by *Bloem, steen* (Flower, Stone) in 1990 and *Waaigat* (Blowhole) in 1993. She won the Halewijn Award for her *oeuvre* in 1998 after publishing her fourth book, *Picknick op de wenteltrap* (Picnic on the Spiral Staircase, 1997). *Hier is de tijd* (Time Is Here, 1998) won the prestigious VSB Poetry Award, followed by *Dakruiters* (Skylights, 2000), winner of the Hugues C. Pernath Prize, and *Alles is nieuw* (Everything Is New, 2005), which was again nominated for the VSB Poetry Award and won the Jan Campert Prize in 2006. She also published her collected poetry, *Altijd vandaag* (Always Today), in 2006, and was awarded the A. Roland Holst Award for her whole *oeuvre*.

Francis R. Jones studied German and Serbo-Croat at Cambridge University and modern Serbo-Croat poetry at Sarajevo University. He is a Senior Lecturer at Newcastle University specialising in translation studies. He mainly translates from Dutch and Bosnian-Croatian-Serbian into English, and has also translated from Hungarian, Russian, French, German and Caribbean Creole languages – and into Yorkshire and Northumbrian dialect. He has won eight international translation prizes, and is the only translator to have won the European Poetry Translation Prize twice: in 1991 for his translation of the Serbian poet Ivan V. Lalić's *The Passionate Measure*, and in 1997 for Lalić's *A Rusty Needle* (jointly with David Constantine's Hölderlin). He was inaugural winner of the James Brockway Prize (2005), the Netherlands' main poetry translation award, mainly for his translations of Hans Faverey (*Against the Forgetting*). His translations of Mak Dizdar's *Stone Sleeper* won him two of Bosnia's top literary awards: a Sarajevo April 6th Prize (1999), and the Bosnia and Herzegovina Association of Publishers and Booksellers' Best Translation Prize (2000).

ESTHER JANSMA

WHAT IT IS
SELECTED POEMS

TRANSLATED BY
FRANCIS R JONES

BLOODAXE BOOKS

ISBN: 978 1 85224 780 5

First published 2008 by
Bloodaxe Books Ltd,
Highgreen,
Tarset,
Northumberland NE48 1RP.

www.bloodaxebooks.com
For further information about Bloodaxe titles
please visit our website or write to
the above address for a catalogue.

Bloodaxe Books Ltd acknowledges
the financial assistance of
Arts Council England, North East.

ACKNOWLEDGEMENT
We wish to thank the Foundation for the Production and Translation
of Dutch Literature for their financial support for this publication.

Cover design: Neil Astley & Pamela Robertson-Pearce.

Printed in Great Britain by
Bell & Bain Limited, Glasgow, Scotland.

CONTENTS

INTRODUCTION

'Heir, myself, collector': the poetry of Esther Jansma

The Dutch poet Esther Jansma has been called 'one of the most important poets of our time'.[1] Her verse interweaves a dazzling diversity of strands. Her mastery of poetic form links the cadences of everyday speech into highly-crafted structures of sound and rhythm. In mood and tone, she balances intensely-felt experience against detached reflection. The philosophical is earthed in the everyday, the mythic intertwines with the mundane, and the word with the world:

> ...The word for lion
> curls and stretches, climbs, crumples.
> Paper consumed by flame; no word
> is big enough for so much
> crude red and gold.
> > ('The word for lion')

Among Esther Jansma's poetic themes, particularly striking is her exploration of time and memory, past and present, death and legacy. This, of course, has been a grand theme of poetry since Gilgamesh and before. But the two opposite yet complementary directions from which she approaches this theme give special power to her verse. One direction draws the poetic essence from her own past and present – from personal tragedies and happinesses, and the scraps and fragments of the everyday:

> Essences, someone said, you find in the smallest
> commonest things, potatoes have gravity too
> > ('Essence of potatoes')

The other direction draws the poetic essence from her second career as research archaeologist, from

> ...what remains of this or another past
> tales and aides-memoire which simply claim
>
> that we were here and nothing more
> in time which existed before today
> > ('Archaeology 2')

In all their diversity, these strands form a complex whole that convinces totally as poetry.

7

What it is

This selection, *What it is*, is the first book-length edition of Esther Jansma's verse to appear in English translation. It aims to introduce the English reader to this most exciting of modern-day Dutch poets, by giving an overview of her poetic output.

In the rest of this introduction, I show how the themes of Esther Jansma's verse twine through each of the collections she has published to date. Then I look at how her verse shapes and is shaped by her use of language. With translated poetry, however, two languages are always present. Hence I finish by describing some of the ways in which the original Dutch became reshaped into English.

Voice Under My Bed

Esther Jansma's debut collection was *Stem onder mijn bed* (*Voice Under My Bed*, 1988). Here, in accessible imagery and subtle poetic tones, Jansma lays down three thematic threads that will underlie all her work. One is the merging of personal experience into a poetic concern with transience and inheritance. Another is the drive to fix or recover the traces of the past before they fade. A third is a vividness of image in which the present instant becomes timeless.

The poems in Esther Jansma's first two collections are written implicitly or explicitly from a first-person viewpoint. Of course, the 'poetic I' in a poem is not necessarily the same as the 'real-poet I' who wrote the poem, as Jansma herself stresses. But the sheer believability of experience and feeling in these two books leads the reader to suspect that the poetic and real-poet I are very close. Hence in the opening poems of *Voice Under My Bed* the adult poetic I recalls her childhood. But the child's eyes are those of a girl who 'learned to disappear' into other worlds, just like the poet and the archaeologist who the real-poet I would become:

> Chipped glass older than me
> could be a coloured curtain
> between the world and my sight.
> How it almost was (blue grass, green light),
> that's what I wanted to remember.
> ('In the back garden')

Through the collection, the child gradually comes of age – until, in 'Archaeology 1', she states her manifesto as poet and archaeologist. This is to be a

8

...collector

of odds and ends, moments,
cracks in things, braille

and so to piece back together the worlds of her personal and our collective past.

Flower, Stone

In her next collection *Bloem, steen* (*Flower, Stone*, 1990), Esther Jansma confronts the reader with the unbearable: the death of one's own child. Built around the experience of stillbirth, this collection was seen at first by critics largely as a personal coming-to-terms, where the main force lies in its raw material – loss, bereavement and survival. But however stark this material, what strikes the reader is this collection's poetic force. As Jansma put it in an interview, her aim was to communicate experience not in the form of self-help manual or diary, but as 'cleansed pure poem'.

Flower, Stone, in fact, is the collection where Jansma finds her mature poetic voice – a voice of both power and control. In terms of poetic form, the stone flowers of the collection's title do not only describe the poet's feelings of bereavement. They also describe the poems themselves, flint knives of compressed image and precisely hewn sound:

> That she was there and then no more
> and what lies in between – tales
> take hold as we retell the told
> all through that night, and again –
>> ('That she was here and then no more...')

In terms of poetic content, the flint knives of Jansma's verse unflinchingly dissect the nature of bereavement and survival. But they also dissect the harsh existential facts of our own life and death which bereavement lays bare. After the lines just quoted, for example, the poetic I's thought-line slices down from her personal here-and-now into the universal, to question with a breathtaking double metaphor the nature of human communication and existence itself:

> as streetlight lays branches bare
> in rings, language lays us out
> round nothing – never letting up,
> head to head, foot to foot
> sounds in a flimsy hoop.

Flower, Stone, therefore, is driven by the poetic I's grief and rage, shaped and honed by Jansma's clinical poetic skill. But it is all of these together that give it such harrowing yet compelling poetic power.

Blowhole

Esther Jansma's next collection *Waaigat* (*Blowhole*, 1993) is much less obviously rooted in real experience than her first two collections. The text-world in which the poetic I now walks is more a world of myth, its workings often less immediately accessible. In the poem 'Schrödinger's catch', a mermaid exists and does not exist in a paradoxical quantum state. And if she crystallises out of this state into life she must die – just as the initial idea, Jansma explains, disappears as it is fixed into the words of a poem. In 'Modernism', laughing friends ride a freeway through a metropolis in the company of angels and unicorns. In 'The word for lion', the word once spoken becomes lion in the speaker's mouth:

> … He licks
> my tongue to bits with his tongue,
> rubs against the bars of my mouth.

And there is the disturbingly imagined 'Son I never had'. In an ironic reversal of what the reader might expect from such a title, he

> Turned out to be a monster with
> the kind of fur found only in the darkness
> under stones…

Moreover, in this collection Esther Jansma's style is even more carefully crafted than before – an issue we will return to shortly.

Time Is Here

Esther Jansma's fourth collection *Hier is de tijd* (*Time Is Here*, 1998) marks both a milestone in her poetic career and a consolidation of her earlier work. Firstly, it confirmed Jansma's growing reputation as a poet of stature. Whereas *Blowhole* had been critically praised, *Time Is Here* won a prestigious national prize – the VSB Poetry Award. Secondly, in this volume Jansma's formal texture has now stabilised into a mature, complex weave which draws its strength from the various stylistic strands of her earlier volumes.

Time Is Here explores, on the one hand, the relationship between perceiver and perceived, the word and the world:

> You are someplace, where does not matter,
> always on a rim, of land and water
> this time, what it tells of is now…
>
> ('This here')

On the other hand, it examines the relationship between past and present, memory and being, death and survival. This is closely linked to Esther Jansma's other career: archaeology. A specialist in dendrochronology, the dating of wooden artefacts from tree-rings, etc., she is leads a research laboratory at the National Service for Archaeology, Cultural Landscape and Built Heritage (RACM) in Amersfoort, and holds a Chair in Dendrochronology and Paleo-Ecology of the Quaternary at Utrecht University.

Time Is Here is the first collection in which she draws inspiration explicitly from this other profession. In 'Archaeology 2', for example, Jansma merges past and present into a single dreamtime where seeing and remembering are one and the same:

> You sit at table. You suddenly see
> someone crossing ice, and how the cold
>
> or some other end overcame him and you say: look,
> here you have his mittens, shoes, and leather cloak.
> 'Where is time? Time is here.'

The dreamtimes in Jansma's historical poems draw both on the detached analysis of the historian and on the imaginative empathy of the poet. These two roles share a common goal. If the task of the historian, in Thomas Carlyle's words, is 'warring against Oblivion', this is also one of the age-old tasks of the poet. Both come together in the purpose Jansma sets herself in many of her poems, whether "personal" or "historical": to document how oblivion gnaws unceasingly at our own personal present, but also to explore the power of personal and collective memory. In this she shows a close affinity with two Dutch master poets of the previous generation, who may be seen as two of her poetic forebears – Hans Faverey and Gerrit Kouwenaar. In the works of these poets, 'stopping time' and reconstructing the past through memory are key themes.

The long poem 'Safe House', which opens *Time Is Here*, explores these themes in a single complex dreamtime that combines the collective and the personal. At first sight, the poetic I is a member of William Barents's and Jacob van Heemskerck's 1596-97 expedition in search of a North-East Passage – a near-mythic national legend of fortitude and survival. His ship crushed by pack-ice, he is sitting out the long winter with his crewmates, marooned in a hut on the island of Nova Zembla in the Arctic Ocean:

> We are somewhere, we can stand, there
> is an above, but dark; the days are short.
> Eating up, using up, burning up
> our ship, we snap at each other like the ice
>
> we drift across like shadows...

But the more one reads, the more one realises that this poem has another, personal layer of meaning – that the Nova Zembla over-wintering may also represent a psychological overwintering. Jansma, in fact, had recently suffered a second terrible loss – the death of her young son. In an e-mail she wrote that

> 'Safe House' is also about having totally lost one's way,
> being icebound, having lost one's language, longing for
> before, for voices which say what has to be done [...], only
> being able to find peace in sleep.

Within *Time Is Here*, a sequence of seven poems stretching from 'Son' to 'Absence' refer most directly to the death of the poet's son. In the original volume, they are not distinguished from the poems that surround them. This suggests that Jansma did not wish to draw attention to their personal inspiration. And yet this sequence is the most moving set of poems I know in modern Dutch poetry. But again, to my mind, this would not be possible if the poet were simply writing out a personal loss. It is the poems' sheer poetic power which moves the reader more deeply than mere rapportage could do. As when, for instance, the bereaved I dreams of release from memory and the words that must speak it:

> and all at once, you growing lighter,
>
> wordlessness happens to fill and lift you up
> till you burst with all that emptiness
> and scatter across the city which in a small
>
> enclosed before, which is quiet, where night,
> where everyone is where they want to be
> and have forgotten themselves and are sleeping
>
> and in that very breath you happen
> to dream: a fleet of paper birds,
> a rustle, there is a way, you can return.
>
> ('New Year')

Here, of course, there are echoes of *Flower, Stone*. But there is a crucial difference between the two books. In *Flower, Stone* Jansma used the raw power of metaphor to wrench the reader from witnessing the unbearable into confronting its wider significance. Though the metaphors still blaze, the poems in *Time Is Here* are more contemplative, using more sustained images in which the personal and the existential are more closely interwoven. With 'Safe House', for example, this means that one cannot simply say that surviving an Arctic winter four centuries ago is "merely" a metaphor, and surviving bereavement is what the poem is "really" about. Image and sub-text, the personal and the collective past are intertwined into one poetic whole.

Skylights

'Absence', which ends the seven-poem sequence just mentioned, is repeated as the first poem of Esther Jansma's next book *Dakruiters* (*Skylights*, 2001), where it opens the new cycle 'Having'. 'Absence', therefore, is a crucial link between the two books. In this edition, rather than printing 'Absence' twice, we chose to keep it just as the first poem of 'Having'– thus keeping the symmetry with 'Presence', the last poem in 'Having'. 'Absence', however, is still the keystone of a single poetic arch. It marks the point at which a personal loss becomes transmuted into a concern with how the tiniest detail contains the universal. In this, 'Absence' has strong echoes of Rainer Maria Rilke's verse – not only in its exquisite compression of imagery and delicacy of tone, but also in the image of the rose itself. This poem is worth quoting in full:

> As roses open, you do not notice,
> a rose is a rose is, is suddenly knowing:
> what was said is saying itself again,
> missing is plural, keeps unfolding into now
>
> and you do not understand how. You lie in the heart
> and wait and nothing seeks you, nothing
> sleeps you into the light, keeps unleafing
> while falling into itself.

In Rilke's poem 'The rose-bowl', a rose's petals are only visible because they angle outwards into infinity. Likewise, the rose of 'Absence' and the second half of the poetic arch echoes both inwards and outwards into infinity. This is because it is a flower of mathematical fractals, which remain the same no matter how many times you zoom in or out:

> In all of her components a rose
> is rose, in every petal she is complete
>
> as this continent's outline is always
> the whole of its coast in each inch
> ('Fractal')

The poems of the arch's second half do indeed seem more mathematical, more philosophical, more detached, at times ironic. Yet the philosophical is also unmistakably the personal. The link lies in the image of the rose. For Rilke, the rose alludes to beauty, the inexpressible, even the world. But for Jansma, the rose also alludes to how these wither in time and remain in dreamtime:

> What fell away till her elements here
> on the table no longer make me think at all of
>
> that rose, that's the rose I think when I say
> I want her back – so, if need be:
>
> non-rose.
> ('A sort of eating')

'Sjaantje and space', the last cycle in *Skylights*, however, reminds us that the personal need not only be experience of loss. Happiness, or the neutral, incidental events in life, can form just as effective material for poetry. As here, where the sense of home experienced by Sjaantje (who might be a girl, or a woman: we do not know) sets wider poetic questions about safety and belonging.

Everything Is New

Proportionally the most poems in this selection are translated from Esther Jansma's most recent collection *Alles is nieuw* (*Everything Is New*, 2005) – a sign, perhaps, that her poetry is still gaining gravitas. Jansma describes the motifs in this book as tracing a double arc. One is an arc gradually moving from the past, firstly collective (such as 'Everything is new') and then of individuals (such as 'A bridge is a door in the road'), and ending with an exploration of present time (from 'The house' to 'In nothing'). The other arc begins with 'everything', the first word in the title of the first poem 'Everything is new', stressing the collective, the common. This second arc ends with 'nothing', the last word in the title of the last poem, that tells how life is an endless fall through the void /

of what we call blue and earth', and that its sense might lie only in 'the humming that's part of it' – in poetry, perhaps.

Several of the poems from the first, historical section were written as part of a project, *Writing on the Wall*, initiated by Arts UK. In this project, poets from the countries that had once garrisoned Hadrian's Wall visited the Wall and wrote their experience into poems.[2] As Esther Jansma is also an archaeologist, she was the obvious poet to invite as a latter-day representative of the Batavians. This is the Germanic tribe who lived in what are now the Dutch provinces of Utrecht and Gelderland, and who are self-deprecatingly satirised in 'AD 128'. And it is just as apt, perhaps, that the resulting poems ('Wall', 'AD 128', 'The collector', 'The beginning' and 'The house') have now been translated and published in Northumberland.

Within this double arc, the topics its poems touch on are varied and lively. In 'Twister', for instance, there is a no-holds-barred poetic counter-attack on elitist, pigeonholing critics. Echoes of tragedy scarred over still remain, as in the poem 'Sheet white'. Underlying many poems, as Jansma points out, is a concern with psychological processes:

> Who has not longed for a mother like a shell
> and then dreamt up a wordless flesh-and-blood
> to fit inside and where the hiss of nothing drowns
> the world?...
>
> ('Metaphysics')

Another frequent feature of these poems is an everyday experience that suddenly reveals existential or numinous depths. Bathing the children, for example, where a small, everyday happiness reveals the fragility of the here and now, as the poetic I

> ...fishes them out of the tub
> tames their arms and legs with a towel she talks
>
> them into pyjamas. And all along she cannot be them
> they're on the point of leaving, are disappearing.
>
> ('Disappearing')

Reaching for potatoes in the kitchen cupboard, as in 'Essence of potatoes'. Or slipping on a snowy street:

> And she always happens just like that
>
> to stand up straight, wipe the snow from her eyes,
> brush herself down, do the usual, buy a paper.
> All things fall towards their end, but how can I
> always know this, at times it slips my mind.
>
> ('What it is 3')

15

This extract shows how, as in many of Esther Jansma's mature poems, she skilfully intertwines the visual and the meditative. This, perhaps, is another way that her work as poet reflects her work as archaeologist. Both involve seeing what is there, envisaging what might have been or might be, and making the resulting picture come alive.

The word and the world: sound and language in Esther Jansma's poetry

In our book-by-book overview of Esther Jansma's work, we have focused on her poetic themes. Her poems, however, are also painstakingly crafted in terms of word-sound and rhythm. Hear, for example, the patterns of alliteration and vowel-rhyme (z, k and short i sounds), and the gentle sprung pentameter, in this original verse from 'This here' (in *Time Is Here*):

> je ligt op je buik. Zand zingt zich voort
> zoals water, geribd. Je kiest de kleinste rib.
> Berg. Je kiest de kleinste korrel. Aarde.

The translation tries to reflect these effects, though English offers a slightly different range of sounds (*aw*, *-l* and short *i*):

> you sprawl on your belly. Sand sings away
> like water, ribbed. You pick the smallest rib.
> Hill. You pick the smallest grain. Earth.

'Archaeology 2' (see above) is another example of Esther Jansma's subtle but total control of form. The conventional rhyme-scheme of the opening stanza seems to reflect this poet's confident pronouncements about a past outside her, but this breaks up into a more irregular pattern of half-rhymes as past and present merge into one.

Here, form echoes content. But in some poems, form becomes content: that is, language becomes what the poem is about. Sound, for example, may be one of a poem's themes. The key to 'The son I never had', Esther Jansma explained on reading my first-draft translation, was the succession of short *o* and *st* sounds running through the poem:

> Bleek een monster met een vacht
> die slechts ontstaan kan in het donker
> onder stenen. Het was een wonder
> dat hij zag dat ik er stond.

We tried to reflect these sound-themes with chains of *st-* and *-nd* sounds in English:

> Turned out to be a monster with
> the kind of fur found only in the darkness
> under stones. It was a wonder
> that he saw me standing there.

In some poems, the relationship between form and content may become the poem's theme. Thus 'The word for lion', from *Blowhole*, describes the relationship between the word 'lion' and the beast that stalks its prey – the prey being the person who speaks it, perhaps. And the bridge the tongue makes to say 'leeuw', Dutch for lion, is also a bridge from which someone might fall to their death:

> With my windswept mouth full of time,
> blowhole, I call the beast and he comes.
> He comes across the billowing bridge
> of my tongue, the arc of an arm which lifts
> above water, then buckles and sinks

The poem 'Uitzicht' from *Time Is Here*, which I translated as 'Swift', takes this theme to a witty extreme. Literally, 'Uitzicht' means both 'View' and 'Outofsight'. The poem as a whole combines the fun of word-play for its own sake with a comment about how, in poetry, the world (what we see) does not only inspire the word (the poem), but the word also creates the poetic world:

>   ...breekt
>
> uit de taal de haas:
> frontaal, waarna
> het staartje t
> zich uit het zicht
> dat dit gedicht is
> haast.

Literally, this means 'the hare breaks out of language: head-on, after which the tail t hurries out of the sight that this poem is'. But the poem's form reflects the content's concern with language. 'Language' ('taal') is physically part of 'head-on' ('frontaal'). The Dutch verb 'hurries' is reflexive: 'zich haast' – literally, 'itself hurries'. Hence, as the hare hurries out of sight ('zicht'), we see its t-shaped tail before we see itself ('zich') – and if we take 'zich' out of 'zicht' we are left with 't'. The hare ('haas') plus its tail 't' makes the verb 'hurries' ('haast'). But 'haast' also means 'almost': the last three lines could also be read as 'out of the sight that this poem almost is'. As I explain below, this also sets the translator a considerable challenge.

Creativity, loyalty and teamwork: translating Esther Jansma

Any book of translated poetry involves two writers: the original poet and the translator. As we have seen in the last section, the message of a good poetic line is deeply rooted in the language in which is it written. Since different languages work differently, this means that a poetry translator cannot simply reproduce a 'source' (original) line's dictionary meaning and its poetic effects – sound-structure, word-play, rhyme and rhythm, etc. He or she has to create a new line that is just as rooted in the new, 'target' language – but ideally one that remains as loyal as possible to what the source poet intended. Balancing creativity and loyalty is the poetry translator's biggest challenge, and each translator's personal balance is different here.

Moreover, the translator is not the only person who shapes the translated text. Poetry translators usually rely on advisors to answer questions about source language problems, cultural allusions and so forth, and to check that the translations work as poetry. When one translates a living poet, the poet is often a crucial advisor. This was particularly the case with *What it is*, which is the product not of a lone translator but of a two-person translating team. Esther Jansma vetted, added to and streamlined my initial choice of poems. And as a skilled English writer herself, as well as being a translator of poetry into Dutch,[3] at every drafting stage she gave close comments and insightful suggestions on my translations, introduction and notes.

Our shared purpose was to give a 'performance' of the original poem which tries to stay as close as possible to the source poet's imagery and style, but which must be poetically convincing in English. These two aims need not rule each other out. But keeping them both in mind makes translating a painstaking yet enjoyable job. As a little case-study, let us look at the opening five lines of 'Archaeology 2':

> Als we ons dan toch moeten kleden,
> tegen kou bijvoorbeeld, of in naam van iets,
> in resten van dit of dat verleden,
> verhalen en geheugensteuntjes die niets
>
> vertellen dan dat we er al waren

Typically, I first analyse and note down the poem's form: in this case, 'irregular sonnet: 1st quatrain full ABAB, rest = ½ rhymes'. I then make a literal English version. This has many alternatives as possible, giving a "bank" of ideas to draw on later:

> If in the end we have to / we have no choice but / we cannot help
>   but dress/clothe ourselves
> against the cold, for instance/example, or in the name of something,
> in remains of this or that past,
> stories/tales and mnemonics/aides-memoire/prompts which say/tell
>   mean
>
> nothing but/beyond that we were [t]here already / have already
>   been here

If the source poem is rhymed, some translators see the rhyme as somehow "separate from" meaning and abandon it in their translations. However, I feel that if rhyme is used, it is *part of* a poem's meaning; and with this particular poem, Jansma pointed out that the gradual disintegration from fixed to looser rhyme scheme through the poem was a crucial feature. Hence rhyme was the main priority in the second draft of 'Archaeology 2'. This turned out as:

> If we have to clothe ourselves anyway
> against the cold, for instance, or in the name
> of something, in some past or other's remnants, say,
> stories and aides-memoire which claim
>
> no more than this: to tell us we already were here

I then revise the draft several times with the aim of creating a viable English poem. The danger, here, however, is that the translation may drift formally or content-wise away from the original. Or both, as in my fourth draft of 'Archaeology 2'. Here, the rhyme-scheme was less tight, and I had added 'same old' to 'stories' for the sake of a rhyme with 'name':

> If we have to dress ourselves anyway,
> against the cold for instance, in something's name,
> or in remnants of whatever past, the same
> old stories and memoranda which tell us no more
>
> than this is where we were before

When I sent this draft to Jansma for comment, she felt that I had lost the crucial ABAB rhyme in the first verse. Hence I checked back with the original and came up with a formally tighter final version:

> If we have to dress, when all is said at last,
> against the cold or in something's name, let's say,
> in what remains of this or another past,
> tales and aides-memoire which simply betray
>
> the fact that we were here, and nothing more

This was then put aside for several months until the whole volume had taken shape. In the final revision phase, Jansma and I talked through the fair-draft volume word by word, in a series of face-to-face meetings and phone calls, negotiating every change. The resulted in the poem's final, slightly tauter version:

> If we have to dress, when all is said at last
> against the cold or in something's name
> in what remains of this or another past
> tales and aides-memoire which simply claim
>
> that we were here and nothing more

With most poems it is possible to reproduce the original form while staying acceptably close to the source-text semantics. But when a poem plays with language itself, as in 'Uitzicht' (described above), the game almost never transfers: 'hare' + 't' in English makes no word at all, never mind both 'hurries' and 'almost'. Here, translators have to decide what is more crucial for the poem in question: to translate the images and lose the word-play, or to make word-plays with totally different words. With 'Uitzicht', I felt that it was more important to reproduce how the play of form sketches a creature almost too quick to be caught by a poem. Hence the Dutch hare became an English swift – which, like *haas*, moves as fast as its name:

> swiftwings flit with a sigh
>
> into sight: then, swifter
> than the telling, a tail
> ineffably
> light in flight v-
> eers out of this
> verse.

This allowed me to reflect what was, to my mind, the underlying purpose of this poem: to show how actions in the world are reflected in the word. Hence *sigh* is both semantically and linguistically *in sight*. And *v* is the swift's *tail* (also its *tale*) which *v-eers* out of this *verse* – semantically by finishing the poem, and linguistically by scattering *verse*'s letters.

For poetry translators, one appeal of translating verse lies in creatively cracking such language puzzles. A more basic appeal is the sheer emotional excitement of engaging closely with poetry that, in Jansma's words, takes us 'beyond the meandering border of this / thinking, the mortared project labelled we'. But the most important motivation of all is the chance to let new readers, in a new language, share this excitement, share the experience of being taken beyond the safe and known, and into the exciting and new. This experience is particularly rewarding when the original poet is not only an artist of freshness and originality, but also of stature and skill. Esther Jansma is such a poet.

FRANCIS R. JONES
Northumberland, April 2008

NOTES

1. Koen Vergeer, 'Riposte to death: Esther Jansma's poetry', in *The Low Countries: Art and Society in Flanders and the Netherlands*, 2001.

2. Collected in *Writing on the Wall* (ed. Steve Chettle, Arts UK, 2006).

3. Most importantly, of the North American poet Mark Strand – whose poetry Jansma sometimes refers to in her own (see Translator's Notes).

ACKNOWLEDGEMENTS

We would like to thank Steve Chettle of Arts UK and Neil Astley of Bloodaxe Books for inspiring this project and bringing us all together. Many thanks are also due to Hanneke Jones-Teuben and Wiljan van den Akker for their close reading, comments and advice on the translations and the Introduction. And thanks too to the late James Brockway and to Paul Vincent, whose translations of certain poems from *Time Is Here* and *Skylights* were gratefully used to improve our own early drafts.

Earlier versions of the following poems appeared in *Irish Pages* (Spring/Summer 2005): 'Safe House', 'This here', 'Swift', 'Son', 'The fall', 'Morning', 'The lovers', 'Tectonics', 'New Year', 'small dream', 'Archaeology 2', 'Absence', 'Fractal', 'A sort of eating', 'Logic in love', 'Outside', 'Potatoes are more important than roses', 'The way we talk', 'Realism', 'Nominalism', 'Arrangements', 'Presence', 'Historical reality', 'Structural survey' and 'Everything is new'.

Earlier versions of the five *Flower, Stone* poems appeared in *Interpoetry* 14 (2006, available at http://www.interpoetry.com/index.html).

Earlier versions of the following poems appeared in *Amsterdam Review* (Summer 2006): 'AD 128', 'In the middle', 'Brain corals', 'The collector', 'Essence of potatoes'.

Earlier versions of these poems appeared on *The Netherlands – Poetry International Web* (2006, available via http://netherlands.poetryinternationalweb.org/piw_cms/cms/cms_module/index.php ?obj_id=4006): 'Absence', 'Fractal', 'Logic in love', 'Presence', 'The collector', 'Everything is new'.

Earlier versions of these poems appeared in *Poetry Wales* (January 2007): 'Nominalism', 'Presence', 'The collector', 'The house'.

Earlier versions of these poems appeared in *Writing on the Wall* (ed. Steve Chettle, Arts UK, 2006): 'The house', 'The beginning', 'AD 128', 'Wall', 'The collector'.

Voice Under My Bed

Stem onder mijn bed

(1988)

Voice under my bed

Just like dust under your bed
that's what they become, he said.
But they don't know they're dead,
he said; they know nothing.

Their fall out of time shoots
past the borders we wake inside
each morning, he said. Beyond
lies nothing, he thought.

You all give your weakness
a voice under your bed and the names
of gods, he said. For he didn't yet
know he was dead.

In the back garden

I soon learned to disappear.
For hours I'd upturn tiles in the yard
and was little, a black insect
in a city of sprouting seeds.

Chipped glass older than me
could be a coloured curtain
between the world and my sight.
How it almost was (blue grass, green light),
that's what I wanted to remember.

But earwigs filled me with fear.
Hiding behind roses, the paper on the wall,
they could crawl inside my ear.

Ghost ship

The child of three who possesses her
mines stone and bronze from old wounds,
remains alone – open mouths of offspring
and awe all round her, it's true,
but no crew.

The thin woman who kneels inside her
speaks to her in sounds
of skin and stone
of fathers who have gone.

Forward glance

When you are dead
I'll take your petroleum lamp.
Then I'll think myself onto a ship,
into a little light, just enough
to write by.

Then everything will end
at my hair on my shoulder,
breathing, the dry sound
of my skin across the sheets,
my pen across the paper
and the bed that moves
with the water.

Archaeology 1

Come back to light
all pasts are like
the soil in which they lay.

The poet I want to be
the rag-and-bone man, collector
of odds and ends, moments,
cracks in things, braille
is forever decoding expressions
of the selfsame face.

*

That she was there and then no more
and what lies in between – tales
take hold as we retell the told
all through that night, and again –

as streetlight lays branches bare
in rings, language lays us out
round nothing – never letting up,
head to head, foot to foot,
sounds in a flimsy hoop.

*

How can you exist in so big a space?
Like a marble in a bowl? I shrink
to the edge, look into the eye
of the moment she shatters.

There are no more pictures of us now,
strata which once existed, or almost.
I am stripped, a small bare world
in a water-cold head.

*

I push crystals, chessboards
of gold, gilded arches and bouquets
out of my head – I replay birth,
I want light to start not in the light
but sooner, turn my fingers round,
furiously press sun, more sun into her eyes.

Dying must be her brightest moment, insane
euphoria. Fall
of a glass acrobat,
sun-pain.

*

There is a space in my head
of silence made by the dead.
I need to speak.

I seek out the biggest sounds,
call stone, for stone always stays itself
and flower, flowers show their true colours.

I also want to grasp that silence
with foot, foot for ever
fixed form in my hands
with such withered little toes.

*

The stone seems to be lying still
but it is falling to the ground
in which she's lying and falling further,
ever more thinly spread; dead
is embracing earth to the core.

And we who stand here now
are taller than ever – however
downwards we look, sink inside our heads:
living on is being hurled upwards,
falling in reverse, weightless.

Blowhole

Waaigat

(1993)

Schrödinger's catch

The mermaid in the gurgling hold
below the fisherman's world
is no longer tangled in invisible
nets of chance, but turning true.

What does she do as she comes into being?
Does she know of the approaching end
and beat her tail and claw her coral nails
to no avail in her world of water?

How afraid is she now the waters give way?

The fisherman turns his boat. 'This evening's
different. See those clouds dangling
like hands above the horizon, the last of
the sunlight flitting between those fingers.
It's strangely still.'

Modernism

This, glass teeth from a lower jaw,
sky-blue palate from which the sun,
that round god of gold, dribbles
its spittle green onto roof gardens
and parkscapes, this is the ideal city.

Here it is early afternoon.
We are all at the wheel, driving
home with constant cries of quiet
delight along the slides of roads.
Like angels in an airport we are

lighter than breath, heedless of technique
like the unicorn nearing the ten-year-old
maiden: glimpse between radiant
planes of concrete, sated hunger for
wholeness, perfection. He leans

towards her lap the way we weave
into the next lane, trembling,
helpless with love for the choreography
that she, almost fitted out,
enacts unknowing, flawlessly.

The word for lion

With my windswept mouth full of time,
blowhole, I call the beast and he comes.
He comes across the billowing bridge
of my tongue, the arc of an arm which lifts
above water, then buckles and sinks

into mirror image. The word for lion
curls and stretches, climbs, crumples.
Paper consumed by flame; no word
is big enough for so much
crude red and gold.

He does not walk, he kills distances.
His scream comes from a stomach of earth,
is a collapse, a deadly slide. He licks
my tongue to bits with his tongue,
rubs against the bars of my mouth.

Burial

Leave the kingdom of rot
where mouths as cold as wax
around the table chew
at what remains of you – hands

flap slow moths around your
skull, love reels upwards like
cigar smoke between the blunt knives
of words – and go into the garden.

They are walking there too. Young,
their thin arms awkward and white.
They do not see you.

Dig yourself a hole and lie inside.
You'll see that time means nothing.
Sometimes you get rained on, that's all.

The son I never had

Turned out to be a monster with
the kind of fur found only in the darkness
under stones. It was a wonder
that he saw me standing there.

Spittle trickled from his mouth.
He could not speak and he was scared;
he saw that things exist outside the cellar
where he'd been shackled fast for years.

He stank, stood stooped,
his hunger huge. I threw my arms
around him. We fell over.

Shaking in the green fur of grass
he started laughing. He's still laughing.
I'm still hoping that he'll stop.

FROM

Time Is Here

Hier is de tijd

(1998)

Safe House

Snow is the felling and falling of giants.
Eardrums beating, screaming trees.
Whispers are water, rafting downriver
to Dordrecht's timber market.

The market is tomorrow, hull and house.
Building is fire and knowledge of stove.
The stove is city. Before is the city
slowing to an etching, soundless, old.

Etched is what you see and cannot grasp:
distance, harbour, house. House is the bark
of the tree that is closing over before,
the ship I live in, where here, now

rain drums, wood groans green, doesn't split
since I am good, my skin my god,
laziness: voice which says we won't,
not us, but Bosnians, Algerians will,

since anyway they'll end up – dead
is reflections of a son gone blind
on a retina racked with thirst.
Thirst is thinking of big water.

Small is dead children, charred people, far away.
Small is news reports, hands, tears are small –
'not even the rain has such small hands'. Hands
are what time falls through on its way like water.

Water is big. Time is big. God too,
so we as well in our womanless belly of wood.
It's cold here. Cold is never being
reborn, so persevering in this here

until things change, scurvy's scarburst gone,
the year that burst and out of which
so much – no more thinking of before.
Noah a hero. Barents a hero.

Heroes trail tales in their wake
like ships. So why this silence?
The splintered figurehead points across
the rock-hard water, there is no rain

we left the rain behind and in its stead
came cold which gnaws our fingers to the bone,
smokes out of our mouths, a glass dragon
that slithered inside us and smothers our words.

We are somewhere, we can stand, there
is an above, but dark; the days are short.
Eating up, using up, burning up
our ship, we snap at each other like the ice

we drift across like shadows, we want to be
what we still know from the dream which is
before: bread, binoculars, windows,
pigeons, children, trees. A wife.

At night I bury myself. At night: a way
back to warmth, flesh, my homeland.
Pissing and shitting as well: a way back
to the crib, the city, lazy days behind

the house, sitting between the flies
on the privy – I still know how to sleep
and shit. I must be almost old now.
I think this white plain in the night

is what old age is about: losing count,
sliding softly down, out of the dream
into a sort of waiting, losing all sense
of where you are, how long, when, what

people are, what wood, hands, what
a place – I still remember a place, it's
ground beneath you and space above you
and being there and knowing why

but this here is beyond me. I am
the others and myself, a knot of skin
sweat sound in endless white
on which I turn my back, I turn around, I

count the hairs in beards, scratch
the scabs off faces, chew on leather,
I want words, to hear what I should do,
first order, second order, commands

are the arteries of this house, rhythm
that fills the void, tell me how
to do it, blood the white
with words like hunting cooking

sawing mending tomorrow next week,
and God just say that God can see this,
say he knows us, that here exists
on charts we are not lost.

Talk so I may know what people
are about. I dream of wood and rain,
hold my hand, comfort me
while I look for walls

while I fall into the belly of sleep
falling is being born again
belly is a safe house
sleep is a rushing awareness of warmth

while I wait for the thaw.

This here

You stroll along the beach: the sea,
the skyline, the sound that fills the bowl
of all the world to the rim – no, smaller.

You press your shoes in the sand: soles,
hills weathered to null, leaving
their print in each other – no, not this.

You are someplace, where does not matter,
always on a rim, of land and water
this time, what it tells of is now – no

you sprawl on your belly. Sand sings away
like water, ribbed. You pick the smallest rib.
Hill. You pick the smallest grain. Earth.

Swift

The way that grand
goes round grassland
and cow lies
in her cowl of flies,
swiftwings flit with a sigh

into sight: then, swifter
than the telling, a tail
ineffably
light in flight v-
eers out of this
verse.

Son

He closes his eyes and the world
unfolds. He falls
while no thing hints at depth

walls collapse, the floor
gives way, air storms in.
Out of time, he plunges down.

Each lullaby is a prologue,
a high voice which sings
holes in his head. Sleep

billows the skirts of the house.
The nest tosses like a ship.
He shivers, clinging on to earth

which his hands, little grapples,
sparrow-talons, knead
from the branches of the sheets.

The fall

We were crossing the Styx.
The ferryman lay drunk in his ship.
I held the helm and we sank like stones.

Water is made like earth
of layers, transparent ribbons, glistening strata
of ever smaller life, less warmth.

Bubbles blossomed in your hair,
the current tugged back your head
and caressed your neck.

Stones waved arms of weed and fern,
sang softly gurgling 'peace'.
They cut away your clothes.

Fish licked the blood from your legs.
I held your hand. I wanted to comfort you
but we were falling too fast and no words exist

without air, my love was left
up above, blue balloons, brief beacons,
marking the site of the accident

before they floated on. Your mouth opened.
Your face turned red, your hands grasped
for balance, grasped for my arms.

You tried to climb me. You were
a glassblower with a cloud of diamonds
at his mouth. I held you like a kitten.

I stroked your fingers.
You did not let go.
You slept and I stroked your fingers, let go.

Morning

Had you lent someone else your face?
Briefly borrowed different eyes? A mouth
for firetalk, watertalk? You sang

to two worlds but were losing this one.
You gripped us tight. Not true,
you lay still and you spoke with ghosts.

Beneath your blankets emptiness opens
her shears. Longing broke into
o's and a's on your lips. Morning light

caught in droplets clings to your
fingers, your cheeks are cold. This is
the moment in which the trees sigh

and unfold and delicate green
creatures flee behind the sparkling
helpless hands which are spiders' webs

leaving us behind, on our retina
the brief shadow of a heel or
a wing, then nothing. Oh elves

are weak, sweetie, and die like mad
while we, we are already forgetting how full
the light once fell on you, how you lie here,

this silent now so full of you, so yourself
and past, so fucking past.

The lovers

Washed ashore, he lay on red rocks
and dreamt her voice was calling him, sand
that was strewn across him and wafted away.

The sea lay still by his breast.
His heart was the nest of colourful
birds. The wind turned back.

One by one the birds took wing,
they screeched and tumbled upwards, helplessly
they were hurled aside.

His heart was a wound, a deserted room
when she found him, the difference between him
and the ground was love, that's all.

She lifted him up. Gently she tried
to close his mouth. In the ship
she tried to close his mouth.

She did not speak and pressed his lips together.
She did not speak and placed his arms around her neck.
It worked. His head lies on her shoulder.

He does not speak. They sail. They mean the world to each other.

Tectonics

Mineral existence, earthship sliding
through strata of earth: I in the hold of we.

Time foams against the ground. The egg
in which one's I follows thin layers

of longing out of the world – it is
a bridal bed, galley where one lashes

oneself as slow as stones to the mast,
stops up one's ears to the sirens, those wispy

fingers of time which prise into the ground
down faults and hairline cracks,

raise the ship, lift the giant numb with I
up and away into the daylight

where everything, living and dead, is merely itself,
bleeds dry on the retina and dies.

New Year

Smoke blows into your mouth. The sun
kicks your hair. Boys in sleeveless shirts
rub the blood from their eyes.

Surgeons polish their instruments
and put them away. Everyone's walking
toward the harbour. You, between the discarded

summer dresses of light, the tatters
and shadows of fireworks, run after them
and all at once, you growing lighter,

wordlessness happens to fill and lift you up
till you burst with all that emptiness
and scatter across the city which in a small

enclosed before, which is quiet, where night,
where everyone is where they want to be
and have forgotten themselves and are sleeping

and in that very breath you happen
to dream: a fleet of paper birds,
a rustle, there is a way, you can return.

small dream

open the doors
sweep the words
out of the house – amazed

up straight in the long
canoe of his sleep
he drifts into your light.

blood, heartbeat,
opening and closing
between your hands

heat-breathing
vase of ribs, in-
florescence, flight of

small round sounds, gentle
rain and a little
red o

Archaeology 2

If we have to dress, when all is said at last
against the cold or in something's name
in what remains of this or another past
tales and aides-memoire which simply claim

that we were here and nothing more
in time which existed before today –
if we can only stay in this now for sure
by constantly inventing ourselves in this now

let's keep it simple, by using clothes.
You sit at table. You suddenly see
someone crossing ice, and how the cold

or some other end overcame him and you say: look,
here you have his mittens, shoes, and leather cloak.
'Where is time? Time is here.'

Skylights

Dakruiters

(2000)

Having

Absence

As roses open, you do not notice,
a rose is a rose is, is suddenly knowing:
what was said is saying itself again,
missing is plural, keeps unfolding into now

and you do not understand how. You lie in the heart
and wait and nothing seeks you, nothing
sleeps you into the light, keeps unleafing
while falling into itself.

Fractal

In all of her components a rose
is rose, in every petal she is complete

as this continent's outline is always
the whole of its coast in each inch

and the slightest wisp of mist
the biggest skyfilling cloud, so

a rose right down to the tiniest
outline of every single petal

and the space suffused with molecules of scent
between these petals is that rose

and does not know it.

A sort of eating

What never knew anything, what painlessly
could have been not itself but say a chair

I can only have it seems
by naming it (a sort of eating)

and so becoming it. A dead whatever
to which I attach myself, a meaning.

What fell away till her elements here
on the table no longer make me think at all of

that rose, that's the rose I think when I say
I want her back – so, if need be:

non-rose.

Logic in love

'Roses' is a different set
than that of what is not called rose

like 'I' and 'alle rozen'. Thinking
on from here in non-logical terms

this flower has to be in disguise
if it is to be with me – for instance I can only

love her in a poem, which a rose is a rose is
something that has long been done

so no set theory here, though one thing is dead
certain: there's room enough for a simple

little rose and me.

Outside

Here there's room for intricate
simplicity to present itself unprompted

since where this is no reflection exists
although so many things are mirrored, there

in the blue black of water for instance
what is leaning across it in leaf red

and skin grey. Gravely by a flowerbed
I think this through: wind and briskness

are everywhere, yet insight is lacking.
It's lucky I am here.

Just look how nature needs me.

Potatoes are more important than roses

except in poems, there roses are more important
whereas it's a delusion to think that tubers

those knobbly starch-packed paunches and pouches
are somehow less lyrical

than vegetable sex organs. Suppose
someone named after a flower is in the ground.

Dead that is. Nothing pretty there. She's decomposing.
I'd sooner stick to potatoes, they don't stink.

And yet – suppose someone who gave her name to a potato
is in the ground. Not only her state but even her name

would be against her. You're better called rose after all.

The way we talk

Those who want to know the named like
themselves love saying names the most.

Brand-new widows and mothers
and royalists are good at this.

They cannot make themselves again
cannot be the unknown child

cannot eat their queen
but her name, they lap it up.

And then there are names that reassure.
Language that points to someone

and this someone exists.

Realism

It already exists before I take a bite
lick it up from the unknown

with new positions of lips and tongue
and a brand-new feeling in my head

let it drop from my mouth and know that now
I'll be bigger and emptier than I was.

But it doesn't need saying
to be what it is: absence

the many ways I miss her
but she does not exist

it is not her.

Nominalism

It is not here until I grant it
a name. I name it rose

and think unnervingly tender eyelids
vein-patterned petals in its wake

and behind that a secret as if
in a baby's fist. That'll be death.

It does not know itself.
It seems to be sleeping

and stays this way while
petal after petal drops

and is lost.

Arrangements

Time, I understand, is a constant wind
in the sails of today, a stiff and die-straight

displacement of now. As if you're in a train
but the view is broader and you're travelling

backwards. Fine. But how a rose can move
so gracefully into the past, grow so gradually balder

in question-mark curls – this I cannot grasp.
Or did I arrange all this myself

because I actually miss it, the sense
of all that is suggested by

question-mark curls?

Presence

I'm done with questions. From now on I'm going
to know things. From now on she is not rose but julia

and her sleep is not the sleep of things.
From now on she can be known, I'm going to live

a long long time with her in a house and feed her,
I'll teach her to speak and she will tell me how it is

while she keeps changing. She keeps using different words.
Sometimes I cut her hair. Then her head changes.

As for me, I change so slowly she won't notice.
When she's grown-up

I'll always have been old and happy.

Historical reality

Now is this reality, this stillness
of warped wood in a worn-out house
which like scorched cookware in glass cabinets
is a weighty matter, made by those who came before?
Or this: they lived stooped over strip fields and wood fires,
lost their teeth young, their children young,
leant on the handles of tools to leer
with toothache-twisted gobs at anything
different (travellers, beautiful women).
Sometimes the disturbing was stabbed with a pitchfork.
They didn't smell good, in fact there was nothing good
about them, they worked themselves to the bone,
believed in god and a myriad intricate sins,
they slaughtered pigs to eat and strangers
to set their head at rest?

Structural survey

This is not the dusk I expected under
the wooden repetition, the inverted wreck
(keel upturned) which is the roof, this is
the dark of ages ago, ages of cattle breathing

in and out, groaning as they shift in the night –
who thought of what back then, who knows?
We measure the rafters, record the carpenter's marks
drill into skylights and purlins, we work

until it is late, we are shadows
who want, no, hope to be more real
than what is here at hand: this wood
and everyone who built with it and is not here.

Sjaantje and space

1

I have a house says Sjaantje a house
like houses you'd hardly even dream of, not
a closed and homely something you can be in
no it's a hole, open on every side

the place in a brown drawing (chalk)
with nothing there. The wind whistles
through but it isn't the wind: it's wishing
you were there. I'm not alone there

maybe this is what I mean maybe it's not
a house at all but a new place, spring
bed of turned earth chalked bold and us
still thin with all the winter in it, ink sketch.

2

It happens says Sjaantje where it all caves in
just as frost breathes wreaths rosettes of ice
summer breathes the hidden microscopic logic
of lichens and moss across it all and this

is where we are. There's night through everything
and it's creaking with what sags, rafters
branches and it's whispering little question marks
mice, inflections, straw and later Sjaantje says

we lay there on our back beneath that broken
roof and it wasn't raining and there were no clouds
no clocks, only knowing we were hanging
there together on the underside of the earth.

3

I'm not moving out says Sjaantje I'm
staying put, I'm used to here, no one
can shift me. I'll sit right here. I'll rest
my head in my hands and wait for winter

but it wasn't for real, of course, you'd come
to save me and I knew it. All along. I was
only playing lonely. You had a flask of tea.
Would you like to play with me. Yes yes yes

we'll wait together till we've turned invisible
under deeper and deeper drifts of dead leaves and till
the frosts come like the winter stores of little creatures
huddled up higgledy-piggledy together we'll lie asleep.

4

I love stones a lot Sjaantje says they stay
and stay and stacked they mark with no mistake
the difference between inside and out. Oh no,
she quickly says, that's what I used to think

when you weren't here and movement didn't count.
Hear that, another plane. And she talks a bit more.
Someone listens, but mainly to her voice. There are
walls and furniture, there'll be a horse outside

but no one thinks of that. Just like in books
it's warm and with a log fire and forever and
unlike in books it's all real, their hands, their hair
all those little screens to hide, to love behind.

Everything Is New

Alles is nieuw

(2005)

Everything is new

What would happen was always there, perfectly
spelt by a cup which shattered, shards
marked with the imprints of thumbs
the shiver-script of pinsharp twigs.

It's not a tale we made up but something
that was here and is here in the traces of ditches
and posts and wood fires long gone cold.
It just needed finding, that's all.

Someone had to look at it and say: what is it
it's this, and there it was, a house with a hearth
people as ever and ever being themselves
the first time in this now and sitting

with warm hands which clasp a cup
by the fire and talking and the tick-tick of rain
is a circle of sound and nothing matters, the night
the invisible clouds, the silence of all

outside that's sleeping or waiting for day
are the roof and the walls round the roof
and the bricks of the house that is already old
but new, being found again today.

Wall

It is the way we say it is, simply
here and us, here in our wide house
built of landscape, grass we understand
and graze, roads, water, fields of grain.

Crystal-clear domains filled with stars and gods
are our roof and here all actions speak for
themselves – and so they must, there is no room
for what is untamed, remains unknown.

And yet beyond the meandering border of this
thinking, the mortared project labelled we, the enemy's
always waiting and I don't know him, he won't fit

inside this head, this order, the nowadays I live in
as if in a night filled with danger and din
and close the windows which keep on blowing open.

AD 128

I come from the mud, with cohorts
up to my eyes in sublunary shite I've razed
forests, repaved and rerouted roads, rebuilt
the Imperial Border. The places I've seen,

pal, soft as porridge the soil there, you drown
in sludge, dine on swill, your billet's a one-arsed
village of sludge slapped into bricks and dried –
not that the bloody sun ever shines there,

it turns its misery-stricken face away,
hides in a slate-grey crying fit of mist
and more vicious, remorseless
pissing rain than you'd believe – but

the crack was good as well. Plenty of blondes,
Batavian whores. Who bleat or is it moo as you
screw them. As for their grasping hard-and-fast
fingers, fair enough, I had the cash.

After that the crossing and work on the wall,
hand of a god who keeps us safe and warm.
The job is done. I stayed on, I live in clover
here in the glow of this stone hand's palm

that reddens as I write. Sunset casts
the shape of old hills on these grasslands,
the clouds above are new, the shades
of night are closing in. I wait.

The escape

Once I must not have known her little white
head inside my head, her small hands
in the shape of mine. That I don't remember.
I look back on myself as always her father.

They say she no longer exists, that by
some event, a few words, a glance, an intent
she has evaporated from today, but she must have
escaped like oil from a lamp which shattered

for I know her and don't I know the world?
Here she belongs and if without her I – at least
let her be the stone at my feet, that tree far off
in the dust of a slope, that dove over there.

The collector

This was not found in some attic but down
at rock bottom like things left after
a modern death, limp neglected tat
in the hands of the heir, myself, collector.

What drives me into the depths is not a desire for
something higher, it's little and insolent, picking up
clothes the dustman left behind – turned to uneven
paving, rain-stained – to know what it was like.

It's rummaging after what vanishes, people
of the past, bits of thinking, sequences
which led to action – the planing of wood

the cutting out of little clothes – moments, long ago
which really were and which really are
vanished till someone holds them, reads them back.

The beginning

Suddenly she saw how wide the world was.
Nothing was the way she had expected
things were fuller than she had thought

and more colourful, by looking through
the glass that had found her she saw
the inside of shells, what moved through it

was form and purely itself and all
the while a rainbow of possibilities
blown into life and lost and found again

after the ages had painted their mother-
of-pearl across it, ever so fragile
there it lay, just like that in her hand.

A bridge is a door in the road

A house is a break in space.
A door is a friendly hole
I can go through to later, to someone.

I'll do that whenever I want.
Whenever I am not six
and no grownup would leave me again.

The roof is the end of looking.
The roof is an upside-down wreck.
The creak of already-old things

the hiss of myself. It is cold.
I find my socks and that helps.
White light, frost-flowers on the panes.

Sheet white

It thought it was gone, but here it lies
in my life again, in the room, on the table
wound in white, small, blind, tangled in

leaving it still moves – this still needs
to learn non-being, slowly to dull
the differences between, say, fingers

head and little neck – this sheet white would
I thought, hold silence, simplicity, nothing.
It echoes on, hatches, empties.

In the middle

The light that points to the edges
to a hand that is not there
and an inkling of plants
and distance, and the white

in between, the luminous
comma of a little arm
the fresh eggshell of a head –
I have it and I want it so.

I'll give up nothing, the darkness
the distance, not the stillness
before it all started moving,
passing, not even the passing.

Disappearing

Someone is bathing the kids and cannot grasp them.
She thinks domains, I space, she space, she
thinks an essence of growing older is youth
feels no longer young but made of rubber or latex

fills her head with the order she loves
their fuss and noise, the monosyllabic
explanations they ask for fishes them out of the tub
tames their arms and legs with a towel she talks

them into pyjamas. And all along she cannot be them
they're on the point of leaving, are disappearing.

Essence of potatoes

It was late and the topic was truth.
Essences, someone said, you find in the smallest
commonest things, potatoes have gravity too

the biggest thing I did in my life so far
was not shouting but waving hi goodbye to all
that vanished and began, the dead, children, everything

changes, let's face it, thermodynamics dictates
that chaos is the rule, everything keeps
moving from whole to broken for good

from this we infer the existence of time, hence
my waving, our waving as well – correction
so far is senseless, the past does not exist

before is a thought, a product, a purchase
so I was not being brave at all, I was only
groping a moment ago in the dark of the cupboard

that is my head for the assumed eternal fact
of tubers bought today and I thought something then
I'd never thought before while doing exactly that.

Shade

We have no dead, we're nothing
but thinking tissues who remember thinking
tissues, make translations like now
you've been dead ten years – ten years

dead does not exist. Those we remember
vanished an aeon as well as a second ago
from their own point of view that is not there.
Totally vanished. So there is no you who is something.

We exist in the shade, the roar of
a wave which is forever just beginning its
fall – all that foam, all that vanishing
in our heads of those who are not there.

Metaphysics

Who has not longed for a mother like a shell
and then dreamt up a wordless flesh-and-blood
to fit inside and where the hiss of nothing drowns
the world? The poet has, he wanted a home.

And now there's only one way out, to shrink her
since he cannot stand the clapped-out
tune the dented wheel of thoughts
inside that head of hers. He is himself.

He slams the hatch of the wire-thin iron belly
shut and hits the road, he takes no god,
his metaphysics is all physical

with death and time and carbon and infinity
enough to make a phrase or two to fit inside
and if not him, then someone else. That shell again.

Twister

Lout on a chain whose every link is the nought
the void of a thought he has not got
o as in impotence first and rot and arsehole later
for o must be filled of course with something copied

filthy on his chain of failings this dipshit
staggers itching pelt of damp trails
of drink and fucking in hope at least –
with women hot for it – louseridden foulmouth

poems need a bit of you-know-what or else the boot
and knocks back another, repeating himself.
That's the way to do it. He's always there, supreme

raffish gapfiller pedagogue toerag rattling
his collecting tin panting for attention
you are nothing his jingle in hope of you're all.

The house

The sounds belong to my ears, the doors
belong to my hands, the red bricks
to my eyes, the floors to my daughters and
the attics to my sons and the other way round

it all belongs to me, I live like I sleep
between the safe walls of my breathing
until the wind shakes them up, forgets
the bricks with my eyes and dies down.

It'll be another wind that's blowing through the house.
Maybe you're still here and maybe not.
It'll be another wind.

Someone has a house, the sounds belong
to her ears, the doors belong to her hands,
but it is not me. We are not there.

What it is

1

It is always today, it is always the house
which is already old, always the man or woman
who looks at the clock, who closes the door and goes
off to sleep, to the city, catches the train

it is always the same one who stays in
the body, regretting the time that is missed
as the end softly settles inside
snow always drifting over the known

wanting to keep it all here, wanting
to have by touch the face of the man or woman
with its tired eyes – it is this house,
the silence here, the white roofs.

2

It is the morning, this window, the hoarfrosted roofs
the chimneys like small cold people breathing
beneath the drift of grey and white, the mothers and fathers
of snow. It is the man who is going off to work.

I see that his hands are too small for his bag.
I run after him with bread and pills. The streets
are like glass, shoppers pass, no one looks surprised
when I fall. The man has long since caught the train.

It is the silence of a million flakes, dizzy
wind-driven doves, a million times I.
It is lying here and spinning with lightness,
turning white, thinking of the man on his way.

3

It always happens just like that, it is falling
and looking into the light where dust in soft
ice-cold dresses tumbles downward and knowing
this cold, these particles all mean nothing.

But the man on the train is wearing his suit.
The train is moving through fields which are white.
That is there at least, thinks the woman lying in the street.
And she always happens just like that

to stand up straight, wipe the snow from her eyes,
brush herself down, do the usual, buy a paper.
All things fall towards their end, but how can I
always know this, at times it slips my mind.

Brain corals

There is a fish, it swims, it took a slew of science
to prove it swims in a dead-straight line
in all its curves it's systematic

I always imagine the depths below
a map, this house of yours and mine and
this one wooden door that's open, this one

I stand in the light of what we call lamp
papers, a chair pushed back aslant
as if someone working there has just stood up
leaving a light curable void behind

and fall (sometime I'll learn to swim) in: the missing
are mine just like my standing in the doorway
from now on a door will be warming my hand

there must be a fish that lives in these brain corals
which does not know where it's heading
and knows this and goes.

In nothing

but the endless fall through the void
of what we call blue and earth
the light glancing off in all directions
down fathomless interstellar chasms
with no ditch, no wooden hoarding
around them, where no one mows the grass
no one thinks we always, the breakers
always, where we keep beating
keep beating our now against the coast
of the black, where there is no roof, the folded
hands of rooftiles and rafters do not exist nor
the space inside, the oak floor of the attic
the chance sound of someone walking
now he's home, the humming that's part of it

TRANSLATOR'S NOTES

Archaeology 1 (28)

In the original collections (*Voice Under My Bed* and *Time Is Here* respectively), 'Archaeology 1' and 'Archaeology 2' were both simply named 'Archaeologie'. The numbers have been added to distinguish them in this edition.

Blowhole / Waaigat (35)

The Dutch word (literally 'blow-gap') means a windy gap, place or hole. In place names, it denotes a windy strait – as with the bay on the Caribbean island of Curaçao (alluded to in 'The word for lion'), or with an island near Nova Zembla to the north of Russia (see note to 'Safe House' below).

Schrödinger's catch (36)

To illustrate a property of quantum physics, Erwin Schrödinger asked the reader to imagine a cat imprisoned inside a soundproof and lightproof box. Inside the box there is a vial of cyanide gas beneath a hammer which is linked to a magnetic switch. A negatively-spinning electron will trip the switch, operating the hammer and killing the cat; but a positively-spinning one will not. During the experiment, one electron of unknown spin passes through the switch. From then on, Schrödinger explained, the cat is both alive and dead, just as the electron has both positive and negative spin. It only becomes one or the other when we open the box, just as the electron only has positive or negative spin once we measure it. Esther Jansma wrote in an e-mail:

> The mermaid is not only tangled in a net (as you would expect with a sea creature) but, in some sort of random process, is becoming more and more probable (and eventually real).

Just as either a dead cat or a live cat crystallises from Schrödinger's box,

> the mermaid in the poem is crystallising into reality (as the poet writes the poem / the reader reads it). In the end, becoming real means existing above the sea, since she has been caught (by the man in the poem, the poet, the reader). To her, existence means dying (sea creatures cannot survive on oxygen). It is a no-win situation, in which there is no easy choice between 'living' or 'dead', unlike in the case of Schrödinger's cat. Either the mermaid does not exist, or she

exists and will die. In the end the mermaid is not caught. So she will not die. But that does not save her, since she will disappear back into the domain of the unrealised. That is also a sort of death.

Burial (39)

'Leave the kingdom of rot' alludes to Mark Strand's line 'Enter the kingdom of rot' from the poem 'Where are the waters of childhood' (*Selected Poems*, 1979). Where in Strand's poem the poetic I finds his derelict childhood house again, here Jansma explains that the poetic I is breaking loose from the childhood home.*

Safe House (42)

This poem alludes to an expedition just as familiar to Dutch readers as Scott's Antarctic expedition is to British readers, and just as emblematic of 'national' virtues of courage and endurance. William Barents and Jacob van Heemskerck led three expeditions in the 1590s in search of a North-East Passage via the North of Russia to the Indies. On their third expedition, the leaders' ship, separated from the rest of the expedition, became trapped in the ice off Nova Zembla (Novaya Zemlya) in September 1596. The men were forced to spend nine months through the polar winter in a hut they had built themselves of driftwood. In June 1597, their ship now crushed by the ice, they set off back to the Netherlands in an open boat. Barents died while they were crossing the sea that now bears his name, but the surviving thirteen returned to a heroes' welcome.

Safe House: The crew took the name of their hut *(Safe House)* from Psalms 31. 2 – 'Be thou my strong rock, for an house of defence to save me.'

Dordrecht's timber market: For a long time the Dordrecht timber market, in the Rhine-Waal delta just upriver from Rotterdam, was one of the main timber markets in the Netherlands. It was thus the main source of wood for the Dutch shipbuilding industry.

not even the rain has such small hands: quoted from E.E. Cummings' 'somewhere i have never traveled, gladly beyond'.

The fall (48)

With gratitude to the late James Brockway, whose earlier version of this poem I used to improve my own.

---

* 'Lenen en stelen' ('Borrowing and stealing'), lecture at University of Groningen, 2007.

New Year (52)

There are intertextual echoes here of lines from Mark Strand's 'The recovery' (in *Darker*, 1970):

> I walked to the water's edge
>
> And saw the doctors wave from the deck of a boat
> That steamed from port, their bags open,
> Their instruments shining like ruins under the moon

small dream (53)

Here again there are intertextual echoes of Mark Strand's 'Where are the waters of childhood':

> Now you invent the boat of your flesh and set it upon the waters
> And drift in the gradual swell, in the labouring salt.
> Now you look down. The waters of childhood are here

Presence (66)

Julia is also the name given to a type of fractal.

Sjaantje and space (69)

With thanks to Paul Vincent for letting me use his earlier version of this poem to improve my own.